Mouth to Mouth

Oral Poems from Around the World

SELECTED BY

John Agard & Grace Nichols

ILLUSTRATED BY

Annabel Wright

WALKER BOOKS
AND SUBSIDIARIES
LONDON · BOSTON · SYDNEY · AUCKLAND

The editors would like to take this opportunity to thank all those scholars and writers for their pioneering work in oral poetries, including Ruth Finnegan, Jerome Rothenberg, Ulli Beier, Jan Knappert, Arthur Waley, Willard R. Trask, C. M. Bowra, Tom Lowenstein, Keith Bosley, Kenneth Rexroth, Denys Thompson, Iona and Peter Opie.

They would also especially like to thank all those anonymous poets from across the world for the gift of their voices.

First published 2004 by Walker Books Ltd
87 Vauxhall Walk, London SE11 5HJ

2 4 6 8 10 9 7 5 3 1

This book has been typeset in Golden Type

Printed in Great Britain by Creative Print and Design (Wales)
Ebbw Vale

British Library Cataloguing in Publication Data:
a catalogue record for this book is available
from the British Library

· ISBN 0-7445-8383-7

www.walkerbooks.co.uk

Contents

What's the News?

If You Love Me

SCHOOL TIME, PLAY TIME

I WISH I COULD TURN INTO SOMETHING

WHAT THE ANIMALS SAID, WHAT THE ANIMALS DID

ON THE ROAD

Buying, Selling, Working

Magic Words and Beginnings

NIGHT THOUGHTS

INTRODUCTION

*E*nter a world when people relied more on memory than on the printed page.

Enter a time when poems weren't written down but said out loud like praise-songs in public places or sung like lullabies in private places.

So much was poetry part of the daily round of life that, according to one old Irish belief, if a barn was infested with rats, you would send for the poet to rhyme away the rats.

This belief in the power of words and the "say-out loudness" of a poem's music can be found among peoples all over the earth. And before their poems were collected into a book, they passed them down for centuries from one generation to another generation. From mouth to mouth.

You too can join in the circle of word-magic. Lull yourself with a lullaby. Repeat a schoolyard chant as you clap and skip. Lend your arm and voice to a work-song. Sing a shanty like a sailor. Riddle yourself

with a riddle. Cry out with the street-
seller. Whisper sweet words with the
lovesick. Cast a spell or curse. But think
twice before you cast, for remember one
Innuit poet warned that "a word spoken by
chance might have strange consequences".

John Agard & Grace Nichols

Ⓦhat's the Ⓝews?

What a Story

Mrs Mason broke a basin,

Mrs Mack heard it crack,

Mrs Frost asked how much it cost,

Mrs Brown said half-a-crown,

Mrs Flory said what a story.

English

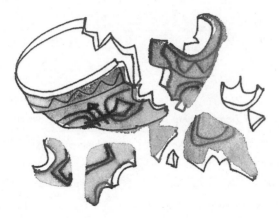

Go tell Aunt Nancy,
Go tell Aunt Nancy,
Go tell Aunt Nancy,
Her old gray goose is dead.

The one she'd been saving,
The one she'd been saving,
The one she'd been saving
To make a feather bed.

She died last Friday,
She died last Friday,
She died last Friday
Behind the old barn shed.

Old gander's weeping,
Old gander's weeping,
Old gander's weeping,
Because his wife is dead.

She's left five little goslings,
She's left five little goslings,
She's left five little goslings
To scratch for their own bread.

American

Flowers Have Come

Flowers have come!
to fresh
and delight you, princes.
You see them briefly
as they dress themselves,
spread their petals,
perfect only in spring –
countless golden flowers!

The flowers have come
to the skirt of the mountain!

Aztec (Mexico)

Yuh walk an talk
A yuh neighbour kitchen door,
An yah bring confusion deh;
Yuh beg a little dis
An yuh beg a little dat,
An yuh bring confusion deh;
Yuh look in a pot
An yuh look out a pot
An yuh bring confusion deh.

Yuh seh Sue seh
An yuh seh Lou seh
An yuh bring confusion deh;
Yuh chat bout Jim
An yuh chat bout Jack
An yuh bring confusion deh.

Yuh look in a hall
An yuh move in a room
An yuh bring confusion deh;
Yuh look pon bed
An yuh look aanda bed
An yuh bring confusion deh.

Jamaican

Riddle

We invited him to come and warm himself
in the sun – he came.
But when we asked him to take his bath,
he said that his death had come.

Answer: Salt

Yoruba (Nigeria)

I Want to Laugh

I want to laugh because my sledge is broken.
Because its ribs are broken, I want to laugh.
Here at Talaviuyaq I struck hummocky ice,
   I met with an upset.
I want to laugh. It is not a thing to laugh at.

Innuit

Ladles and jelly spoons:
I come before you
To stand behind you
And tell you something
I know nothing about.

Next Thursday,
Which is Good Friday,
There'll be a mothers' meeting
For fathers only.

Wear your best clothes,
If you haven't any.
And if you can come,
Please stay at home.

Admission free;
Pay at the door.
Take a seat
And sit on the floor.

It makes no difference where you sit;
The man in the gallery is sure to spit.

American / English

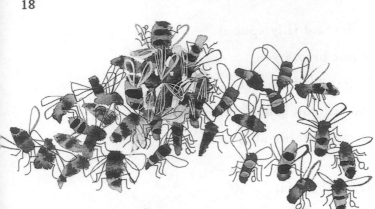

Fog

A fog from the sea
Brings honey to the bee;
A fog from the hills
Brings corn to the mills.

English

Coming Winter

Onion skin,
Very thin,
Mild weather coming in;
Onion skin thick and tough,
Coming winter cold and rough.

English

Braw News Is Come to Town

Braw news is come to town,
Braw news is carried;
Braw news is come to town,
Jean Tamson's married.

First she got the frying pan,
Then she got the ladle,
Then she got the young man
Dancing on the table.

Scottish

Jemmy Dawson

Brave news is come to town,
Brave news is carried;
Brave news is come to town,
Jemmy Dawson's married.

First he got a porridge-pot,
Then be bought a ladle;
Then he got a wife and child,
And then he bought a cradle.

English

I have news for you: the stag bells,
  winter snows, summer has gone,
Wind high and cold, the sun low,
  short its course, the sea running high.
Deep red the bracken, its shape is lost;
  the wild goose has raised its accustomed cry.
Cold has seized the birds' wings;
  season of ice, this is my news.

Irish

A Young Lady's Horoscope

You'll be rich – or you'll be poor.
You'll store meat for the New Year.
Of your parents, one is male
and the other is female.
When you marry, your baby
will be a girl – or a boy.

Vietnamese (translated by Keith Bosley)

News

When the rich man is pricked by a thorn
   the whole city knows;
when the poor man is bitten by a snake
   the event is unrecorded.

Proverb, Lebanese (Arabic)

Sun, Moon, Stars

Sun, moon, stars,
You that move in the heavens,
Hear this mother!
A new life has come among you.
Make its life smooth.

From a ceremony for the newborn, Omaha (Native American)

If You Love Me

There Was a Lady Loved a Swine

There was a lady loved a swine,
Honey, quodth she,
Pig-hog, wilt thou be mine?
Hoogh, quodth he.

I'll build thee a silver sty,
Honey, quodth she,
And in it thou shalt lie.
Hoogh, quodth he.

Pinned with a silver pin,
Honey, quodth she,
That you may go out and in,
Hoogh, quodth he.

Wilt thou have me now,
Honey? quodth she.
Speak or my heart will break.
Hoogh, quodth he.

English

He gave me a quince,

I gave him a jade pendant,

Not in repayment,

But to make our love lasting.

He gave me a peach,

I gave him an emerald,

Not in repayment,

But to make our love lasting.

He gave me a plum,

I gave him black jade,

Not in repayment,

But to make our love endure.

Chinese

Hark, pretty girl, to whatever I ask,
and answer my questions from first to last.
Where lies a water where no fish swim?
Where stands a house and no table within?

You foolish fellow, you downright dunce!
Your noggin hasn't a grain of sense!
In deep well-water no fish swim;
when a house is empty, no table's within.

Hark, pretty girl, to what I ask,
and answer my questions from first to last.
Where's there a king without a land?
Where is there water without any sand?

You foolish fellow, you downright dunce!
Your noggin hasn't a grain of sense!
The king a card game has no land;
the water of eyes is without any sand.

Hark, pretty girl, to whatever I ask!
And answer my questions from first to last.
What rises higher than a house?
What moves more nimbly than a mouse?

You foolish fellow, you downright dunce!
Your noggin hasn't a grain of sense!
The chimney is higher than the house;
the cat is nimbler than the mouse.

Hark, pretty girl, to whatever I ask!
And answer my questions from first to last.
Where's there a tailor with no shears, none?
Where's there a soldier without a gun?

You foolish fellow, you downright dunce!
Your noggin hasn't a grain of sense!
A tailor who's dead has no shears, none;
a soldier discharged is without a gun.

Hark, pretty girl, to whatever I ask!
And answer my questions from first to last.
What's deeper than the deepest spring?
What's bitterer than a hornet's sting?

You foolish fellow, you downright dunce!
Your noggin hasn't a grain of sense!
The sea is deeper than the deepest spring;
Death's deeper than a hornet's sting.

Yiddish (Poland)

Do You Carrot All for Me?

Do you carrot all for me?
My heart beets for you,
With your turnip nose
And your radish face.
You are a peach.
If we cantaloupe,
Lettuce marry;
Weed make a swell pear.

American / English

The New Law

Come here, beloved,
Come give me a kiss.
There is a new law
which says we must embrace each other.

Zulu (South Africa)

Mr Frog went a-courtin', he did ride,
Ahum, ahum.
Mr Frog went a-courtin', he did ride,
Took a pistol by his side,
Ahum, ahum.

He rode up to Miss Mice's door,
Ahum, ahum.
He rode up to Miss Mice's door,
Said, Miss Mice, won't you marry me?
Ahum, ahum.

Where shall the wedding supper be?
Ahum, ahum.
Where shall the wedding supper be?
Way down yonder in an old holler tree,
Ahum, ahum.

What shall the wedding supper be?
Ahum, ahum.
O, what shall the wedding supper be?
Sweet potato and a roasted flea,
Ahum, ahum.

American

Love Song

First, I admire you for your hair
  dressed like a rooster's tail.
Second, I love you because you speak
  so charmingly.
Third, I love you for your features,
  which are sweet to look at.
Fourth, I love you for your clothes,
  which are all the same colour.
Fifth, I love you because you have pins in your
  hair and a Chinese Fan in your hand.
Sixth, I love you because your hair is green.
Seventh, I love you because your parents
  brought you into the world.
Eight, I love you because your phoenix eyes
  look at me most lovingly.
Ninth, I love you because we are going to be
  married and live together.
Tenth, I love you because you will not marry
  anyone but me.

Vietnamese

As I did the washing one day
Under the bridge at Aberteifi,
And a golden stick to drub it,
And my sweetheart's shirt beneath it –
A knight came by upon a charger,
Proud and swift of broad of shoulder,
And he asked if I would sell
The shirt of the lad that I loved well.

No, I said, I will not trade –
Not if a hundred pounds were paid;
Not if two hillsides I could keep
Full with wethers and white sheep;
Not if two fields full of oxen
Under yoke were in the bargain;
Not if the herbs of all Llanddewi,
Trodden and pressed, were offered to me –
Not for all the likes of that, I'd sell
The shirt of the lad that I love well.

Welsh (translated by Tony Conran)

Lullaby

It's my fat baby,
I feel in my hood,
Oh, how heavy he is!
Ya ya! Ya ya!

When I turn my head,
He smiles at me, my baby,
Hidden deep in my hood,
Oh, how heavy he is!
Ya ya! Ya ya!

How pretty he is when he smiles
With his two teeth, like a little walrus!
Oh, I'd rather my baby were heavy,
So long as my hood is full.

Innuit

O Shannadore, I love your daughter,
Hi-oh, you rolling river,
I'll take her 'cross the rolling water,
Ah-hah, I'm bound away 'cross the wide
  Mizzoura.

For seven years I courted Sally,
Hi-oh, you rolling river,
For seven more I longed to have her,
Ah-hah, I'm bound away 'cross the wide
  Mizzoura.

She said she would not be my lover,
Hi-oh, you rolling river,
Because I was a dirty sailor,
Ah-hah, I'm bound away 'cross the wide
  Mizzoura.

A-drinkin' rum and a-chewin' t'baccer,
Hi-oh, you rolling river,
A-drinkin' rum and a-chewin' t'baccer,
Ah-hah, I'm bound away 'cross the wide
  Mizzoura.

Sea shanty, American

I beg of you, Chung Tzu,

Do not climb into our homestead,

Do not break the willows we have planted.

Not that I mind about the willows,

But I am afraid of my father and mother.

Chung Tzu I dearly love;

But of what my father and mother say

Indeed I am afraid.

I beg of you, Chung Tzu,

Do not climb over our wall,

Do not break the mulberry-trees we have planted.

Not that I mind about the mulberry-trees,

But I am afraid of my brothers.

Chung Tzu I dearly love;

But of what my brothers say

Indeed I am afraid.

I beg of you, Chung Tzu,

Do not climb into our garden,

Do not break the hard-wood we have planted.

Not that I mind about the hard-wood,

But I am afraid of what people will say.
Chung Tzu I dearly love;
But of all that people will say
Indeed I am afraid.

Chinese (translated by Arthur Waley)

SCHOOL TIME, PLAY TIME

The Milk-Tooth Mouse

Mishka-mishka,
Mousey mouse,
In a corner of the house,
Find the baby tooth I lost.
It's left a gap just where I bite –
Give me another, strong and white!

Russian

Boys and Girls Come out to Play

Boys and girls come out to play,
The moon doth shine as bright as day,
Leave your supper and leave your sleep,
And come with your playfellows into the street.

Come with a whoop, come with a call,
Come with a goodwill or not at all.
Up the ladder and down the wall,
A half-penny roll will serve us all.
You find milk, and I'll find flour,
And we'll have a pudding in half-an-hour.

English

Who will you marry?
Rich man, poor man,
Beggar man, thief.
Rich man, poor man,
Beggar man, thief.

What will you dress in?
Silk, satin,
Flour bag, rice bag.
Silk, satin,
Flour bag, rice bag.

What shoes will you wear?
High heels, low heels,
Long boots, barefoot.
High heels, low heels,
Long boots, barefoot.

How are you getting to the church?
Hire car, lorry,
Bicycle, dray cart.
Hire car, lorry,
Bicycle, dray cart.

Where will you live when you marry?
Upstairs, downstairs,
Kitchen or coop.
Upstairs, downstairs,
Kitchen or coop.

Where will you sleep?
Spring bed, hammock,
Mattress, floor.
Spring bed, hammock,
Mattress, floor.

How many children will you have?
One, two, three, four, five,
Six, seven, eight, nine ...
One hundred and ninety-nine...

Guyanese (South America)

Riddle

An old green witch
stands in her ditch.
Your hand will hurt
if you touch her skirt.

Answer: Nettle

Swedish (translated by Siv Cedering)

Cape Cod

Cape Cod girls have no combs,
They comb their hair with codfish bones.

Cape Cod boys, they have no sleds,
They slide down dunes on codfish heads.

Cape Cod doctors have no pills,
They give their patients codfish gills.

Cape Cod cats, they have no tails,
They lost them all in sou'east gales.

American

You're daft, you're potty, you're barmy,
You ought to join the army.
You got knocked out
With a brussels sprout.
You're daft, you're potty, you're barmy.

Cowardy, cowardy custard,
Fell in his mother's mustard.
The mustard was hot,
He swallowed the lot,
Cowardy, cowardy custard.

English

Onward, upward may we ever go,

Day by day in strength and beauty grow,

Till at length each of us may show

What Guyana's sons and daughters can be.

A verse from one of the national songs of Guyana

(Children's Version)

Onward, upward, Mary had a goat,

Day by day she tied it with a rope,

Till at length de goat burst de rope

And Mary had to run behind it.

While shepherds watched their flocks by night
All seated on the ground
An angel of the Lord came down
And glory shone around.

Christmas carol, English

(Children's Version)

While shepherds washed their socks by night
All seated round the tub
A bar of Sunlight soap came down
And they began to scrub.

Two rice cakes

On the food tray are quarrelling.

Two large ants

In the honey bottle

Are fighting.

Two balls of earth

On the pondside are wrestling.

You drain my pond

I dry yours up!

Your basket's full of fish

Mine's full of shrimp.

You go to market,

So do I.

You sell cakes before the Temple,

I sell before the King's Palace.

You make shrimp sauce,

I make fish sauce,

You're your father's daughter,

I'm my father's son.

You're the eldest,

I'm the second youngest.

You wear a round basket,

You wear a conical hat.

You hold scissors,

I hold a knife.

What you do

I do the like.

Children's game, Vietnamese

Ladybird

Lady, Lady, Landers,
Lady, Lady, Landers,
Take up your cloak
About your head,
And fly away
To Flanders.
Fly o'er firth,
And fly o'er fell,
Fly o'er pool,
And running well,
Fly o'er moor

And fly o'er mead,
Fly o'er living,
Fly o'er dead,
Fly o'er corn,
And fly o'er lea,
Fly o'er river,
Fly o'er sea,
Fly o'er east,
Or fly you west,
Fly to him
That loves me best.

Scottish

54 ## Good Day, Mrs Monday

Good Day, Mrs Monday!
How is Mrs Tuesday?
Quite well, Mrs Wednesday.
Please tell Mrs Thursday
that myself and Mrs Friday
will be coming next Saturday
for cake with Mrs Sunday.

Folk tradition, German (translated by Bettina Smith)

Chi-chi, Tom Tit

Chi-chi, tom tit,
Where are you going to, tom tit?
To steal a bit of hemp seed.
What if the farmer sees?

I'll fly and hide in the pine tree.

And what if you go hungry?

I'll peck at the pine cones.

What if they stick in your gullet?

I'll poke and I'll pull them out.

And what if you start bleeding?

I'll dip in the water and wash.

And what if your wings are frozen?

I'll light a fire for warmth.

And what if the fire starts spreading?

I'll stamp and I'll put it out.

And what if you break your leg then?

I'll find a smith to mend it.

And what if you can't find one?

I'll find a tinker to mend it.

And what if you can't find one?

I'll go and find Alatyr.

And what if you can't find him?

I'll go to Simbirsk to get mended.

And what if you can't find Simbirsk?

Then I'll stamp and I'll stamp and I'll throw myself

Straight into the trap!

Chuvash (former USSR)

Bate, Bate, Chocolate

Bate, bate, chocolate,

Tu nariz de cacahuate.

Uno, dos, tres, CHO!

Uno, dos, tres, CO!

Uno, dos, tres, LA!

Uno, dos, tres, TE!

Chocolate, chocolate!

Bate, bate, chocolate!

Bate, bate, bate, bate,

Bate, bate, CHOCOLATE!

Mexican

Stir, stir, chocolate,

Your nose is a peanut.

One, two, three, CHO!

One, two, three, CO!

One, two, three, LA!

One, two, three, TE!

Chocolate, chocolate!

Stir, stir, the chocolate!

Stir, stir, stir, stir,

Stir, stir, CHOCOLATE

Awakening the Fingers

You, thumb there, wake up!
The kayak-rowers are about to leave you!
Forefinger there, wake up!
The umiak-rowers are about to leave you!
Middle finger there, wake up!
The wood-gatherers are about to leave you!
Ring-finger there, wake up!
The berry-gatherers are about to leave you!
Little finger there, wake up!
The crake-heather-gatherers are about to
   leave you!

Innuit

I Wish I Could Turn into Something

I wish I could turn into something:

Turn into a nightingale,

And learn the nightingales' language;

I'd come to dwell in the garden.

I'd gather up golden bouquets,

Dip them in liquid silver,

I'd come to you in the evening,

And lay them out on your roof.

When you come out in the morning,

May they be entwined in your curls!

Georgian

Sometimes I feel like a motherless child,
Sometimes I feel like a motherless child,
Sometimes I feel like a motherless child,
A long ways from home,
A long ways from home.

Sometimes I feel like I'm almost gone,
Sometimes I feel like I'm almost gone,
Sometimes I feel like I'm almost gone,
A long ways from home,
A long ways from home.

Sometimes I feel like a feather in the air,
Sometimes I feel like a feather in the air,
Sometimes I feel like a feather in the air,
And I spread my wings and I fly,

I spread my wings and I fly.

Spiritual, African-American

I Sometimes Think

I sometimes think I'd rather crow
And be a rooster than to roost
And be a crow. But I dunno.

A rooster he can roost also,
Which don't seem fair when crows can't crow.
Which may help some. Still I dunno.

Crows should be glad of one thing, though;
Nobody thinks of eating crow,
While roosters they are good enough
For anyone, unless they're tough.

There are lots of tough old roosters though,
And anyway a crow can't crow,
So mebby roosters stand more show.
It looks that way. But I dunno.

American

I wish I was a little grub
With whiskers round my tummy.
I'd climb into a honey pot
And make my tummy gummy.

English

Wishing Myself into a Turtle

There was a storm once.

That's when I wished myself

into a turtle.

But I meant on land!

The one that carries a hard tent

on his back.

I didn't want to be floating!

I wanted to pull everything inside

and dry.

Here comes the waves

shaking me,

And I'm getting sick in the insides.

I wanted to be the turtle

eating buds and flowers and berries.

I've got to wish things exactly!

That's the way it is

from now on.

Swampy Cree (Native American)
(translated by Howard A. Norman)

Two sisters who had no brother
Made one of silk to share,
Of white silk and of red.
For his waist they used barberry wood,
Black eyes, two precious stones.
For eyebrows sea leeches.
Tiny teeth a string of pearls.
They fed him sugar and honey sweet.
And told him: now eat and then speak.

Serbian (translated by Charles Simic)

Woke into a Heron

She was tall, you could see her
in the distance before anyone.

Once, in late summer,
she stood so long at the edge
of the swamp
we thought she was ready
to leave with the herons.

You could see her standing
very still.

The day the herons left
she stayed. The next day she woke as a girl
all right, but she began being a HERON!
She took long steps, slowly, as if she was
walking in water, hunting in water.
This is true, and she did this
making heron noises.

AND had thin sticks
tied out from her feet
to make heron tracks.

This went away
the next morning. Everyone
was happy she would no longer
go sleep in the water reeds.

This was the first time we saw someone
do this, so we named her
not to forget it.

Swampy Cree (Native American)
(translated by Howard A. Norman)

If You Can

If you can walk
you can dance.
If you can talk
you can sing.

Zimbabwean

There Was a Young Farmer of Leeds

There was a young farmer of Leeds
Who swallowed six packets of seeds.
It soon came to pass
He was covered with grass,
And he couldn't sit down for the weeds.

English

I Have Changed

Pamba hufanyiwa nyuzi
nyuzi hufanyiwa shuka
usikumbuke ya juzi
mwingine nimegeuka.

Cotton is made into threads;
Threads are made into a veil;
Do not remember the things of yesterday;
I have changed into someone else.

Swahili (Africa)

WHAT THE ANIMALS SAID,
WHAT THE ANIMALS DID

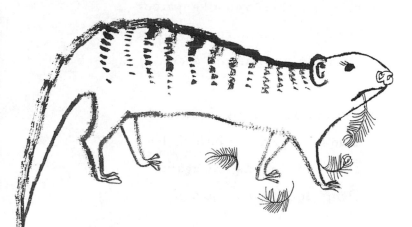

In come de animals two by two,

Hippopotamus and a kangaroo.

Dem bones gonna rise again.

Dem bones gonna rise again.

In come de animals three by three,

Two big cats and a bumble bee.

Dem bones gonna rise again.

Dem bones gonna rise again.

In come de animals four by four,

Two thru de window and two thru de door.

Dem bones gonna rise again.

Dem bones gonna rise again.

In come de animals five by five,

Almost dead and hardly alive.

Dem bones gonna rise again.

Dem bones gonna rise again.

In come de animals six by six,

Three with clubs and three with sticks.

Dem bones gonna rise again.
Dem bones gonna rise again.

In come de animals seven by seven,
Four from Hell and de others from Heaven.
Dem bones gonna rise again.
Dem bones gonna rise again.

In come de animals eight by eight,
Four on time and de others late.
Dem bones gonna rise again.
Dem bones gonna rise again.

In come de animals nine by nine,
Four in front and five behind.
Dem bones gonna rise again.
Dem bones gonna rise again.

In come de animals ten by ten,
Five big roosters and five big hens.
Dem bones gonna rise again.
Dem bones gonna rise again.

African-American

Sly Mongoose

Sly mongoose

Dog know yuh ways.

Sly mongoose

Dog know yuh ways.

Mongoose went in de lady kitchen

Pick up one of she big fat chicken

Put in he waist-coat pocket.

Sly mongoose.

Folk song, Caribbean

Kookaburra

Kookaburra sits on the old gum tree,

Merry merry King of the bush is he,

Laugh, Kookaburra, laugh, Kookaburra,

Gay your life must be.

Kookaburra sits on the old gum tree,

Eating all the gumdrops he can see,

Stop, Kookaburra, stop, Kookaburra,

Leave some there for me.

Australian

Beware of the one who has sharp weapons
And wears a tiger-tail tuft,
Of him who has white dogs,
O son of the short-haired lioness!
You my short-haired child,
Son of the lioness who devours raw flesh,
You flesh-devourer!
Son of the lioness whose nostrils are red
  with bloody prey,
You with blood-reddened nostrils!
Son of the lioness who laps up swamp water,
You water-lapper.

Southern African

Butterfly

O glistening one
O book of God
O learned one
Open your book!

Praise poem, Hausa (Africa)

78   *Riddle*

From far away it cries, it moans, it asks for help;
Yet when it approaches, a slap is
what it receives.

Answer: Mosquito

Filipino

Who killed Cock Robin?
"I," said the Sparrow,
"With my bow and arrow,
  I killed Cock Robin."

Who saw him die?
"I," said the Fly,
"With my little eye,
  I saw him die."

Who caught his blood?
"I," said the Fish,
"With my little dish,
  I caught his blood."

Who'll make the shroud?
"I," said the Beetle,
"With my thread and needle,
  I'll make the shroud."

Who'll dig his grave?
"I," said the Owl,
"With my spade and trowel,
  I'll dig his grave."

Who'll be the parson?
"I," said the Rook,
"With my little book,
    I'll be the parson."

Who'll be the clerk?
"I," said the Lark.
"I'll say Amen in the dark;
    I'll be the clerk."

Who'll be chief mourner?
"I," said the Dove,
"I mourn for my love;
    I'll be chief mourner."

Who'll bear the torch?
"I," said the Linnet,
"I'll come in a minute,
    I'll bear the torch."

Who'll sing his dirge?
"I," said the Thrush,
"As I sing in the bush,
    I'll sing his dirge."

Who'll bear the pall?
"We," said the Wren,
  Both the Cock and the Hen,
"We'll bear the pall."

Who'll carry his coffin?
"I," said the Kite.
"If it be in the night,
  I'll carry his coffin."

Who'll toll the bell?
"I," said the Bull,
"Because I can pull,
  I'll toll the bell."

All the birds of the air
  Fell to sighing and sobbing
When they heard the bell toll
For poor Cock Robin.

American / English

The Centipede

The centipede was happy
Until the toad, for fun,
Said, "Hey, which leg goes after which?"
Which worked his mind to such a pitch
He lay down sadly in a ditch,
Wondering how to run.

English

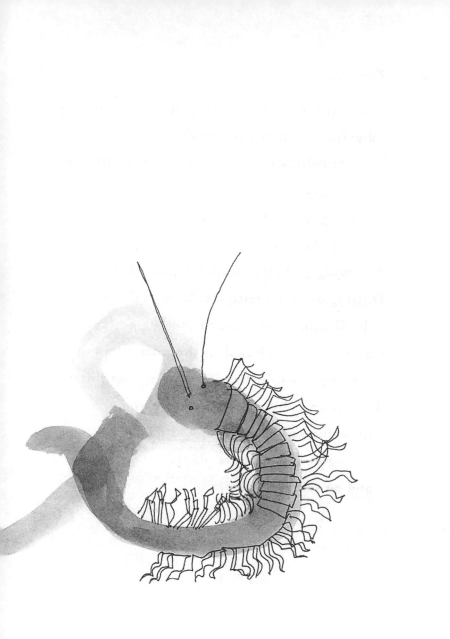

The prawn is there, at the place of the Dugong,
  digging out mud with its claws...
The hard-shelled prawn living there in the water,
  making soft little noises.
It burrows into the mud and casts it aside
  among the lilies...
Throwing aside the mud, with soft little noises...
Digging out mud with its claws at the place of
  the Dugong, the place of the Dugong's Tail...
Calling the bone bukalili, the catfish bukalili,
  the frog bukalili, the scared tree bukalili...
The prawn is burrowing, coming up,
  throwing aside the mud, and digging...
Coming up to the lotus plants
  and on to their pods...

Moon Bone Cycle, Aborigine (Australia)

The mackerel's cry
Is "Never long dry!"

English

The Codfish and the Hen

The codfish lays a thousand eggs,
The homely hen lays one.
The codfish never cackles
To tell you what she's done.
And so we scorn the codfish
While the humble hen we prize.
Which only goes to show you
That it pays to advertise.

American

Duck

Duck, you are merely boasting,

You have borne children.

But you have no back to carry them!

Duck, you are merely boasting.

Children's song, Yoruba (Nigeria)

Sparrow

Pardal pardo porque pairas?
Eu pairo e pairarei
Porque sou o pardal pardo,
Parlador d'el-rei.

Yellow Sparrow, why d'you prattle?
I prattle and prattling I will
Because I'm the yellow sparrow,
Royal prattler of King Will.

Tongue-twister, Portuguese
(remembered and translated by Francisco Manso)

The Cock and the Vixen

Vixen, you're out early
In this nasty weather –
– No, friend, none too early
When you think what I'm out for.
In my right cheek here
I've a tooth that's killing me.
If you would pull it for me,
I'll do you some other favour –

– Close your eyes, then, vixen –
And the cock flew onto the roof-tree.
– *Cock-a-doodle, come down, come down!*
Come down, cock crow! –
– The first time that you caught me
You pulled out all my tail,
And the next time you won't leave me
With a whole bone in my body!

Spanish (translated by W. S. Merwin)

Song of a Bear

There is danger where I move my feet.
I am whirlwind. There is danger
  when I move my feet.
I am a gray bear.
When I walk, where I step
  lightning steps from me.
Where I walk, one to be feared.
Where I walk long life.
One to be feared I am.
There is danger where I walk.

                               Native American

I Know, You Know, We All Know

Out the little rabbit goes
to the market to do the shopping.
I know, you know, we all know –
what he's going to get.

He bought a big cabbage
and a fresh lettuce.
I know, you know, we all know –
big and juicy

He bought a bunch of carrots
because his wife likes them.
I know, you know, we all know –
very tender.

But his house is very small
with all these vegetables and joys.
I know, you know, we all know –
nothing fits.

And so his wife bawls him out.
It's not for nothing they call Mrs Rabbit –
I know, you know, we all know –
a yeller.

But can I tell you what Mr Rabbit does?
He's so stubborn –
I know, you know, we all know –
he plays deaf.

Greek (remembered and translated by Eleni Markouli)

ON THE ROAD

Song

Today is the day I must leave,
I will not go today, I will go tomorrow.
You will see me set out playing on
  a fly-bone flute,
carrying a spider-web for a flag;
my drum will be an ant's egg
and my hat! My hat will be a
  hummingbird's nest.

Quechua (Peru)
(translated by Mark Strand)

"Now, pray, where are you going?" said
 Meet-on-the-Road.
"To school, sir, to school, sir," said Child-as-
 it-Stood.

"What have you in your basket, child?" said
 Meet-on-the-Road.
"My dinner, sir, my dinner, sir," said Child-
 as-it-Stood.

"What have you for dinner, child?" said
 Meet-on-the-Road.
"Some pudding, sir, some pudding, sir," said
 Child-as-it-Stood.

"Oh, then, I pray, give me a share," said
 Meet-on-the-Road.
"I've little enough for myself, sir," said Child-
 as-it-Stood.

"What have you got that cloak on for?" said
 Meet-on-the-Road.
"To keep the wind and cold from me," said
 Child-as-it-Stood.

96 "I wish the wind would blow through you,"
       said Meet-on-the-Road.
    "Oh, what a wish! What a wish!" said Child-
       as-it-Stood.

    "Pray, what are those bells ringing for?" said
       Meet-on-the-Road.
    "To ring bad spirits home again," said Child-
       as-it-Stood.

    "Oh, then I must be going, child!" said Meet-
       on-the-Road.
    "So fare you well, so fare you well," said
       Child-as-it-Stood.

                                          English

I am waiting at the crossroads.

I look to the right –

there is nothing.

I look to the left –

there is nothing.

I look straight ahead –

there is silence.

I take the guinea pepper in mouth.

I recite the old incantations.

I walk a little while – I see calabash.

I break it – there is a crown of brass.

I want to pick it – it says "No!

But you may ask for six things."

I say, you crown of brass,

let me have money,

  wife,

    child,

      health,

        victory,

let me return to try another life.

                Magic formula, Yoruba (Nigeria)

A Ride on a Tiger

There was once a young lady of Riga
Who went out for a ride on a tiger:
They returned from the ride
With the lady inside
And a smile on the face of the tiger.

English

Hello, sir, hello, sir.
Meet you at the show, sir?
No, sir. Why, sir?
Because I've got a cold, sir.

Where'd you get the cold, sir?
At the north pole, sir.
What were you doing there, sir?
Catching polar bears, sir.

How many did you catch, sir?
One, sir, two, sir, three, sir, four, sir, five, sir,
Six, sir, seven, sir, eight, sir, nine, sir, ten, sir.
All the rest were dead, sir.

How did they die, sir?
Eating apple pie, sir.
What was in the pie, sir?
A big fat fly, sir.

What was in the fly, sir?
A big fat germ, sir.
What was in the germ, sir?
A big fat you, sir!

Australian

Song of Two Ghosts

My friend
This is a wide world
We're travelling over
Walking on the moonlight.

Pawnee (Native American)

Riddle

As I walked along the road
I saw a black thing in a furrow,
Neither flesh nor neither bone,
Yet it had four fingers and a thumb.

Answer: Glove

English

If along the highroad
I caught hold of your sleeve,
Do not hate me;
Old ways take time to overcome.

If along the highroad
I caught hold of your hand,
Do not be angry with me;
Friendship takes time to overcome.

Chinese, seventh century BC
(translated by Arthur Waley)

The Butterfly Messenger

I asked a butterfly,

I sent a dragonfly,

to go out to see my mother,

to go out to see my father.

The butterfly came back,

the dragonfly came back,

saying, your mother is crying,

saying, your father is suffering.

I went myself,

I took myself there,

and it was true my mother was crying,

and it was true my father was suffering.

Quechua (Peru)
(translated by Mark Strand)

A man with a hat on, I say no;
How should I know he is bald,
Bald, bald, nothing but bald,
Yes, indeed, nothing but bald?

A man with trousers on, I say no;
How should I know he is bow-legged,
Bow-legged, bow-legged, nothing but
  bow-legged,
Yes, indeed, nothing but bow-legged?

A man with glasses on, I say no;
How should I know he has a squint,
A squint, a squint, nothing but a squint,
Yes, indeed, nothing but a squint?

A man with shoes on, I say no;
How should I know his toes have jiggers,
Jiggers, jiggers, nothing but jiggers,
Yes, indeed, nothing but jiggers.

                        Malawi (Africa)

Myself

As I walked by myself
And talked to myself,
Myself said onto me,
"Look to thyself,
Take care of thyself,
For nobody cares for thee."

I answered myself,
And said to myself,
In the selfsame repartee,
"Look to thyself,
Or not look to thyself,
The selfsame thing will be."

English

Mother! Mother! My boat is sinking,
  here in the ocean of this world:
Fiercely the hurricane of delusion
  rages on every side!
Clumsy is my helmsman, the mind:
  stubborn my six oarsmen, the passions:
Into a pitiless wind
I sailed my boat, and now it is sinking!
Split is the rudder of devotion:
  tattered is the sail of faith.
Into my boat the waters are pouring!
  Tell me, what shall I do?
For with my failing eyes, alas!
  Nothing but darkness do I see.
Here in the waves I will swim,
O Mother, and cling to the raft of Thy name!

Bengali

Mother's Song

If snow falls on the far field
where travellers
spend the night,
I ask you, cranes,
to warm my child in your wings.

Japanese

Buying, Selling, Working

De Ah-Got-Um Man . . . . African-American

Sweet Blooming Lavender . . . . English

Cockles and Mussels . . . . Irish

I Had a Nickel . . . . American

Day Da Light . . . . Jamaican

Wooden Whistle . . . . American / English

Hunger . . . . Yoruba (Nigeria)

Trading . . . . American

Father Grumble . . . . American / Scottish

Ah got pompanos!
Ah got catfish!
Ah got buffaloes!
Ah got um!
Ah got um!

Ah got stringbeans!
Ah got cabbage!
Ah got collared greens!
Ah got um!
Ah got um!

Ah got honeydew!
Ah got can'lopes!
Ah got watermelons!
Ah got um!
Ah got um!

Ah got fish!
Ah got fruits!
Ah got veg, yes 'ndeed!
Ah got any kind o' vittles!
Ah got anything yo' need!

Ah'm de Ah-Got-Um Man!

African-American

Come, all you young ladies,
  and make no delay.
I gathered my lavender fresh
  from Mitcham today.

Will you buy my sweet
  blooming lavender?
There are sixteen dark blue
  branches a penny.
You buy it once,
  you will buy it twice.
It will make your clothes
  smell sweet and nice.
Who'll buy my sweet
  blooming lavender?
Sixteen full branches
  a penny.

London street cry, English

In Dublin's fair city
Where the girls are so pretty,
I first set my eyes on sweet Molly Malone.
She wheeled her wheelbarrow
Through streets broad and narrow,
Crying, "Cockles and mussels, alive, alive, oh!"

Alive, alive, oh!
Alive, alive, oh!
Crying, "Cockles and mussels, alive, alive, oh!"

She was a fishmonger,
But sure 'twas no wonder,
For so were her father and mother before.
And they both wheeled their barrow
Through streets broad and narrow,
Crying, "Cockles and mussels, alive, alive, oh!"

Alive, alive, oh!
Alive, alive, oh!
Crying, "Cockles and mussels, alive, alive, oh!"

She died of a fever,

And none could relieve her,

And that was the end of sweet Molly Malone.

But her ghost wheels her barrow

Through streets broad and narrow,

Crying, "Cockles and mussels, alive, alive, oh!"

Alive, alive, oh!

Alive, alive, oh!

Crying, "Cockles and mussels, alive, alive oh!"

Folk song, Irish

I Had a Nickel

I had a nickel and I walked around the block.

I walked right into a baker shop.

I took two doughnuts right out of the grease;

I handed the lady my five-cent piece.

She looked at the nickel and she looked at me,

And said, "This money's no good to me.

There's a hole in the nickel, and it goes right through."

Says I, "There's a hole in the doughnut, too."

American

114   *Day Da Light*

Day O, Day O,
Day da light an mi waan go home.
Come Missa Tallyman
Come tally mi banana
Day da light an mi waan go home.

Mi deh ya today
Mi may not come tomorrow
Mi come ya fi wuk
Me no come ya fi idle
No gimme such a load
Mi no horse wid bridle
Day da light an mi waan go home
Six hand, seven hand, eight hand bunch,
Day da light an mi waan go home.

De checker dem a-check
But dem check wid caution
Mi back dissa bruk
Wid sheer exhaustion
Day da light an mi waan go home.

Day O, Day O,

Day da light an mi waan go home.

Come Missa Tallyman

Come tally mi banana

Day da light an mi waan go home.

Folk song, Jamaican

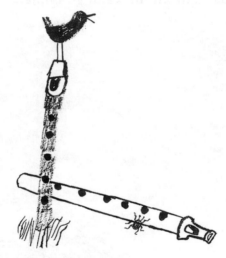

Wooden Whistle

I bought
a wooden
whistle,
but it
wooden
whistle.

I bought
a steel
whistle,
but it
steel
wooden
whistle.
So
I bought
a tin
whistle.
And now
I tin
whistle!

American / English

Hunger

Hunger is beating me.

The soapseller hawks her goods about.

But if I cannot wash my inside,

How can I wash my outside?

Masquerader's chant, Yoruba (Nigeria)

Trading

Went to the river, couldn't get across,

Paid five dollars for an old gray hoss.

Hoss wouldn't pull so I traded for a bull.

Bull wouldn't holler so I traded for a dollar.

Dollar wouldn't pass so I threw it on the grass.

Grass wouldn't grow so I traded for a hoe.

Hoe wouldn't dig so I traded for a pig.

Pig wouldn't squeal so I traded for a wheel.

Wheel wouldn't run so I traded for a gun.

Gun wouldn't shoot so I traded for a boot.

Boot wouldn't fit so I thought I'd better quit.

So I quit.

American

There was an old man lived under the hill,
As you may plainly see, see.
He said he could do more work in a day
Than his wife could do in three, three,
He said he could do more work in a day
Than his wife could do in three.

"Be it so, then," the old lady replied,
"But this you must allow,
  That you go work in the house today
  And I'll go follow the plow.

"But you must milk the Teeny cow,
  For fear that she goes dry.
  And you must feed the little pigs
  That live in yonder sty.

"You must watch the speckled hen
  For fear she lays away.
  And you must wind the hank of yarn
  Your wife spun yesterday.

120   "You must go to the dining-room
          And scour up all the plates;
          And don't forget the curly dog,
          Or he'll eat all of the cakes.

       "You must wash the dirty clothes
          That hang upon the wall;
          But don't forget the crooked stairs
          Or you'll get an awful fall.

       "You must churn the crock of cream
          That stand upon the frame;
          But don't forget the fat in the pot
          Or 'twill all go up in a flame."

          So the old woman she took the whip in her hand
          To go and follow the plow,
          And the old man he took the pail on his arm
          To go and milk the cow.

          But Teeny she hooked, and Teeny she crooked,
          And Teeny turned up her nose;
          And then she gave the old man such a kick
          That the blood ran down to his toes.

He went to watch the speckled hen
For fear she'd lay away;
But he forgot to wind the yarn
His wife spun yesterday.

He then went to the dining-room
To scour up all the plates;
But he forgot the curly dog,
And he ate all of the cakes.

He went to wash the dirty clothes
That hung upon the wall;
But he forgot the crooked stairs,
And he got an awful fall.

He went to churn the crock of cream
That stood upon the frame;
But he forgot the fat in the pot,
And it all went up in a flame.

That night he swore by the light of the moon
And all the stars in heaven
His wife could do more work in a day
Than he could do in seven.

American / Scottish

MAGIC WORDS AND BEGINNINGS

Rain Chant

Dad a da da

Dad a da da

Dad a da da

Da kata kai

Ded o ded o

Ded o ded o

Ded o ded o

Da kata kai

Aborigine (Australia)

WHILE *washing the hands in the moon's rays*
shining in a dry metal basin, recite the following:

I wash my hands in this thy dish,

Oh man in the moon, do grant my wish,

And come and take away this.

English

Spell to Get Rid of Hiccups

I have the hic,

I have the swallow.

I give it to someone else

Who can cope with it.

Children's rhyme, Dutch (Netherlands)

Steal not this book for fear of shame,

For in it is the owner's name;

And if this book you chance to borrow,

Return it promptly on the morrow.

Or when you die the Lord will say,

Where's that book you stole away?

And if you say you do not know,

The Lord will answer, Go below!

English

Oh our Mother the Earth, oh our Father the Sky,

Your children are we, and with tired backs

We bring you the gifts that you love.

Then weave for us a garment of brightness;

May the warp be the white light of morning,

May the weft be the red light of evening,

May the fringes be the falling rain,

May the border be the standing rainbow.

Thus weave for us a garment of brightness

That we may walk fittingly where birds sing,

That we may walk fittingly where grass is green,

Oh our Mother the Earth, oh our Father the Sky!

Tewe (Native American)

Spell to Summon Money

Pay me a visit!

Pay me a visit!

O Money, pay me a visit!

I'm living in this town.

Pay me a visit!

Yoruba (Nigeria)

Midwife's Song to Ayopechtli

In her house of clouds
in cloud banners, liquid necklaces
in water, mist, somewhere.

Somewhere life
in ripe wombs.

Up! Come up!
Let yourself
be sent,
come out,
come,

child, feather
sub-
feathery marine
being.

Come up, come

up, come
be born, jewel child
come up,
come

Here!

                              Aztec (Mexico)

Amairgin's Spell to Bespell Fish

Fishful the sea!
Fruitful the land!
A fountain of fish!
Fish under wave
Like a torrent of birds,
A crowded sea!

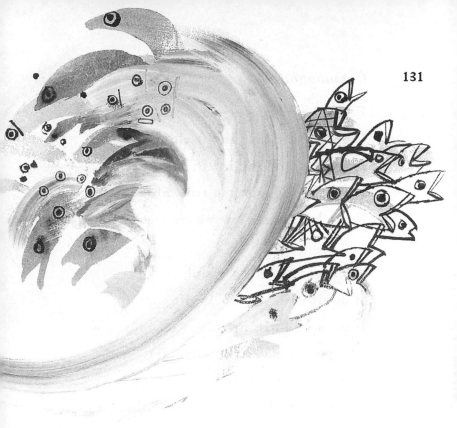

A white hail
Of countless salmon,
Of broad-mouthed whales!
A harbour spell –
A fountain of fish,
A fishful sea!

Irish (translated by Caitlin Matthews)

From the conception the increase,

From the increase the swelling,

From the swelling the thought,

From the thought the remembrance,

From the remembrance the consciousness, the desire.

The word became fruitful;

It dwelt with the feeble glimmering;

It brought forth night;

The great night, the long night,

The lowest night, the loftiest night,

The thick night, to be felt,

The night to be touched, the night unseen,

The night following on,

The night ending in death.

From the nothing the begetting,

From the nothing the increase,

From the nothing the abundance,

The power of increasing, the living breath;

It dwelt with the empty space,

It produced the atmosphere which is above us.

The atmosphere which floats about the earth,
The great firmament above us, the spread
  out space dwelt with early dawn,
Then the moon sprung forth;
The atmosphere above dwelt with the glowing sky,
Forthwith was produced the sun,
They were thrown up above as the chief eyes
  of Heaven:
Then the Heavens became light,
The early dawn, the early day, the mid-day.
The blaze of day from the sky.

The sky which floats above the earth,
Dwelt with Hawaiki...

                    Maori (New Zealand)

This fig tree is her staff, folks say.

Destroy it not in any way.

Upon it lays a dreadful curse,

Who plucks a leaf will need a hearse.

English

BEFORE being destroyed in a gale, a fig tree
once grew from the wall at St Newlyn Church near
Newquay in Cornwall. Whoever took a leaf or
a fig from it was said to die within a year.

May those who love us, love us,

and those who don't love us,

may God turn their hearts.

And if he doesn't turn their hearts,

may he turn their ankles

so we will know them by their limp.

Irish

May they stumble, stage by stage
On an endless pilgrimage,
Dawn and dusk, mile after mile,
At each and every step, a stile;
At each and every step withal
May they catch their feet and fall;
At each and every fall they take
May a bone within them break;
And may the bone that breaks within
Not be, for variation's sake,
Now rib, now thigh, now arm, now shin,
But always, without fail, THE NECK.

Welsh (translated by Robert Graves)

The Fishermen's Prayer

Protect me, O Lord,
My boat is so small,
And your sea is so big.

Protegez moi, mon Seigneur,

Ma barque est si petite,

Et votre mer est si grande.

Old Breton (France)

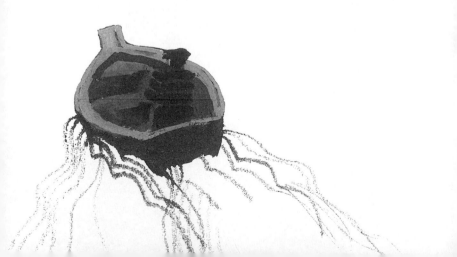

Come, Rain, Come Pouring Down

Come, rain, come pouring down
I'll measure out the paddy now.
Come, raindrops, gather on the horizon
In this wood-cracking burning heat of day.
Come, rain, come pouring down.
Come, rain, come pouring down.

Aye brishti jhepe

Dhan debo mepe

Aye rimjhim barosharo gagane

Kathphatha rode agune

Aye brishti jhepe ayere.

Aye brishti jhepe ayere.

Bengali (remembered and translated by Bashabi Fraser)

The Sun Is My Mother

The sun is my mother,
The moon is my father,
The twinkling stars
Are my sister and brother.

Georgian (translated by Kevin Tuite)

Ned Flaherty's Curse on the One Who Murdered His Beautiful Drake (extract)

May his pig never grunt,
  may his cat never hunt,
May a ghost ever haunt
  him at dead of the night,
May his hen never lay,
  may his ass never bray,
May his goat fly away
  like an old paper kite,
That the flies and the fleas
  may the wretch ever tease,
May the biting north breeze
  make him shiver and shake,
Bad wind to the robber
  be he drunk or sober,
That murdered Ned Flaherty's
  beautiful drake.

May his pipe never smoke,
   may his tay-pot be broke
And to add to the joke
   may his kittle ne're boil,
May he stick to the bed
   till the hour that he's dead,
May he always be fed on
   hogwash and boiled oil,
May he swell with the gout,
   may his grinders fall out,
May he roll, howl and shout
   with the horrid toothache,
May his temple wear horns,
   and the toes many corns
Of the monster that murdered
   Ned Flaherty's drake.

                              Irish

May it be delightful my house;

From my head may it be delightful;

To my feet may it be delightful;

Where I lie may it be delightful;

All above me may it be delightful;

All around me may it be delightful.

Navajo (Native American)

I am:

The Camel that brings wealth,

The Land that breeds the Ngwu tree,

The Performer in the period of youth,

The Back that carries its brother,

The Tiger that drives away the elephants,

The Height that is fruitful,

Brotherhood that is mystic,

Cutlass that cuts thick bushes,

The Hoe that is famous,

The Feeder of the soil with yams,

The Charm that crowns with glory,

The Forest that towers highest,

The Flood that can't be impeded,

The Sea that can't be drained.

Ibo (Africa)

NIGHT THOUGHTS

Coorie doon, coorie doon, coorie doon,
  ma daurlin', Coorie doon the day,
Coorie doon, coorie doon, coorie doon,
  ma daurlin', Coorie doon the day.

Lie doon, ma dear, and in your ear,
  tae help you close your eye,
I'll sing a song, a slumbering song,
  a miner's lullaby.
Your daddy's doon the mine, ma daurlin',
  doon in the Curly Main,
Your daddy's howkin' coal, ma daurlin',
  for his wee wean.

Coorie doon, coorie doon, coorie doon,
  ma daurlin', Coorie doon the day,
Coorie doon, coorie doon, coorie doon,
  ma daurlin', Coorie doon the day.

There's daurkness doon the mine,
  ma daurlin', daurkness, dust and damp,
But we must hae oor heat, oor light,
  oor fire and oor lamp.
Your daddy coories doon, ma daurlin',
  doon in a three foot seam,
So you can coorie doon, ma daurlin',
  coorie doon and dream.

Scottish

I met my big brother,
Sleep
and he asked me:
What are you carrying on your back?
I answered: the moon.

The moon is very sad.
I asked her:
Where is happiness?
and she answered:
Happiness is with others.

I carried the moon on my back,
and I walked and I wept.
Moon, you are hungry,
you are sleepy,
all of nature shivers with cold.

I met Sleep,
and he asked me
what I carried on my back.

I answered that I carried
nothing but the moon,
and he said:
Rock her to sleep, rock her to sleep.

Berber (North Africa)
(translated by Rabiaa El Maloumi)

My Dress Is Old

My dress is old, but at night the moon is kind,
Then I wear a beautiful moon-colored dress.

Native American

Alone in the Greenwood

Alone in the greenwood must I roam,
Hollin, green hollin,
A shade of green leaves is my home,
Birk and green hollin.

Where nought is seen but boundless green,
Hollin, green hollin;
And spots of far blue sky between,
Birk and green hollin.

A weary head a pillow finds,
Hollin, green hollin,
Where leaves fall green in summer winds,
Birk and green hollin.

Enough for me, enough for me,
Hollin, green hollin,
To live at large with liberty,
Birk and green hollin.

Scottish

Hush, Little Baby, Don't Say a Word

Hush, little baby, don't say a word,
Papa's gonna buy you a mocking-bird.

And if that mocking-bird won't sing,
Papa's gonna buy you a diamond ring.

If that diamond ring turns to brass,
Papa's gonna buy you a looking-glass.

If that looking-glass gets broke,
Papa's gonna buy you a billy goat.

And if that billy-goat falls down,
You'll still be the sweetest little baby
    in town.

                              African-American

Fire-fly Song

Flitting white-fire insects!
Wandering small-fire beasts!
Wave little stars about my bed!
Weave little stars into my sleep!
Come, little dancing white-fire bug,
Come, little flitting white-fire beast!
Light me with your white-flame magic,
Your little star-torch.

Ojibwa (Native American)

The Sweetest Thing

There is in this world something
that surpasses all other things
in sweetness.
It is sweeter than honey
it is sweeter than salt
it is sweeter than sugar
it is sweeter than all
existing things.
This thing is sleep.
When you are conquered by sleep
nothing can ever prevent you
nothing can stop you from sleeping.
When you are conquered by sleep
and numerous millions arrive
millions arrive to disturb you
millions will find you asleep.

Soussou (Africa)

At a time when the earth became hot
At a time when the heavens turned about
At the time when the sun was darkened
To cause the moon to shine
The time of the rise of the Pleiades,
The slime, this was the source of the earth
The source of the night that made night
The intense darkness, the deep darkness
Darkness of the sun, darkness of the night
Nothing but night.
The night gave birth...

                                        Hawaiian

Nothing

Blessed is the girl with nothing at all,
Never a worry where to hide it all;
Sleeps so tightly,
Wakes up sprightly,
Nothing to steal, not a bean, nor a ball!

Czech (translated by Andrew Fusek Peters and Vera Fusek Peters)

Acknowledgements

"What a Story", "Cock Robin", "There Was a Lady Loved a Swine" and "Boys and Girls Come out to Play" are taken from *The Opie Book of Nursery Rhymes*, published by Puffin; "The Old Gray Goose" and "In Come de Animals Two by Two" are taken from *The Faber Book of Popular Verse*, edited by Geoffrey Grigson, published by Faber & Faber Ltd; "Yuh Walk an Talk" and "Day Da Light" are taken from *Mango Walk: Jamaican Folksongs and Games*, published by Jamaica Publishing House Ltd; "Riddle", "Duck", "Luck", and "Hunger" are taken from *Yoruba Poetry* by Ulli Beier, published by Cambridge University Press, 1970; "I Want to Laugh" is taken from *Primitive Song* by C. M. Bowra, published by Mentor; "Ladles and Jelly Spoons", "Do You Carrot All for Me?" and "I Had a Nickel" are taken from *A Rocket in My Pocket*, compiled by Carl Withers, published by Henry Holt and Company; "Fog" is taken from *Weather Lore* by Richard Inwards, published by Charles River Books; "Coming Winter" is taken from *Origins of Rhymes, Songs and Sayings* by Jean Harrowven, published by Pryor Publications; "Braw News Is Come to Town" and "Alone in the Greenwood" are taken from *The Hogarth Book of Scottish Nursery Rhymes*, edited by Norah and William Montgomerie, published by Vintage; "Jemmy Dawson" and "A Ride on a Tiger" are taken from *The Faber Book of Nursery Verse*, edited by Barbara Ireson, published by Faber & Faber Ltd; "This Is My News" is taken from *Celtic Mysteries* by John Sharkley, 1975, and reprinted by kind permission of Thames & Hudson Ltd; "Sun, Moon, Stars" is taken from *Dancing Tepees*, selected by Virginia Driving Hawk Sneve, published by Holiday House Inc.; "The Quince" is taken from *The White Pony: An Anthology of Chinese Poetry*, edited by Robert Payne, published by Mentor Books; "Answer My Questions from First to Last" is taken from *A Century of Yiddish Poetry*, edited by Aaron Kramer, published by Cornwall Books, reproduced by permission of Associated University Presses; "The New Law" is taken from *Around the World in Eighty Poems*, published by Macmillan Publishers Ltd; "Love Song" and "The Sweetest Thing" are taken from *Distant Voices*, edited by Denys Thompson, published by Heinemann Educational Books Ltd; "The Shirt of a Lad" is taken from *Welsh Verse*, translated by Tony Conran, published by Seren, Wales 1992; "The Wide Mizzoura" is taken from *The American Songbag* by Carl Sandburg and is reprinted by kind permission of Harcourt Publishers Ltd; "I Beg of You Chung Tzu" is taken from *Chinese Poems*, compiled by Arthur Waley, published by Allen & Unwin; "The Milk-Tooth Mouse" is reproduced from *Sheep Don't Go to School*, edited by Andrew Fusek Peters, Translation © 1999 Michael Bird, reproduced by permission; "Skipping Rope Wedding Chant" and "Versions" are remembered by John Agard and Grace Nichols; "Riddle" (Nettle), translated by Siv Cedering, is taken from *World Poetry*, edited by Katharine Washburn and John S. Major, published by W. W. Norton & Co. Inc.; "Cape Cod" is taken from *A World of Poetry*, selected by Michael Rosen, published by Kingfisher Publications; "What You Do I Do" is taken from the *Parabola Journal: The Magazine of Myth and Tradition*; "Good Day, Mrs Monday", translated by Bettina Smith, is taken from *Was Kinder gerne hören*, edited by Theo Riegler, published by Bertelsmann 1965; "Chi-chi, Tom Tit" is taken from *An Anthology of Chuvash Poetry*, translated by Peter France, published by

published by Puffin; "Spell to Get Rid of Hiccups" is taken from *Spells and How They Work* by Janet and Stewart Farrar, published by Robert Hale Ltd; "Charm to Protect a Book" is taken from *I Saw Esau*, edited by Iona Opie, published by Walker Books; "Midwife's Song to Ayopechtli" is taken from *Flower and Song: Aztec Poems*, translated by Edward Kissam and Michael Schmidt, published by Anvil Press Poetry, 1977; "Amairgin's Spell to Bespell Fish" is taken from the *Encyclopedia of Celtic Wisdom*, edited by Caitlin and John Matthews, published by Rider. Used by permission of the Random House Group Ltd; "St Newlina's Staff" is taken from *The Puffin Book of Magic Verse*, edited by Charles Causley, published by Puffin; "Ned Flaherty's Curse on the One Who Murdered His Beautiful Drake" is taken from *The Second Book of Irish Ballads* by James N. Healy, published by Ossian Publications Ltd; "I Am" is taken from *Oral Literature in Africa*, edited by Ruth Finnegan, published by Clarenden Press, 1970; "Miner's Lullaby" is taken from *The Scottish Folksinger*, edited by Norman Buchan and Peter Hall, published by HarperCollins Publications Ltd, reprinted by permission of PFD on behalf of Peter Hall and The Estate of Norman Buchan, © 1971 Peter Hall and Norman Buchan; "Amazigh Lullaby" is taken from *Ninna Nanna*, performed by Montserrat Figueras, produced by Alia Vox; "My Dress Is Old" is taken from "Little Indians Speak" from *The Gift is Rich* by E. Russell Carter, published by Holiday House Inc.; "Hush Little Baby, Don't Say a Word" is taken from *The Keskidee Queen*, edited by Faustin Charles, published by Blackie Children's Books; "At a Time" is taken from *Beginnings: Creation Myths of the World* selected and arranged by Penelope Farmer, published by Chatto & Windus Ltd; "Nothing" is reproduced from *Sheep Don't Go to School*, edited by Andrew Fusek Peters, published by Bloodaxe Books Ltd.